COUNTRY

Formal Name: The constitution of December 15, 1999, changed the name of the country from the Republic of Venezuela (República de Venezuela) to the Bolivarian Republic of Venezuela (República Bolivariana de Venezuela).

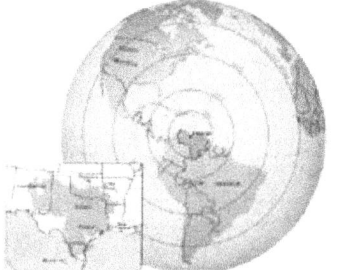

Click to Enlarge Image

Short Form: Venezuela.

Term for Citizen(s): Venezuelan(s).

Capital: Caracas.

Major Cities: Caracas, 1.8 million inhabitants; Zulia, 2.9 million; and Carabolo, 1.9 million (2003).

Independence: July 5, 1811, from Spain.

Public Holidays: Año Nuevo (New Year's Day), January 1; Carnaval (Carnival), the Monday and Tuesday before Ash Wednesday, movable dates in early February to early March; Día de San José (St. Joseph's Day), March 19; Jueves Santo (Holy Thursday) and Viernes Santo (Holy Friday), movable holidays in March or April; Signing of Independence, April 19; Primero de Mayo (Labor Day), May 1; Ascension, May 20;* Corpus Christi, June 10;* Sagrado Corazón (Sacred Heart), June 18;* Battle of Carabobo, June 24; San Pedro y San Pablo (Saint Peter and Saint Paul), June 29;* Firma Acta de Independencia (Signed Act of Independence), July 5; Battle of Boyacá, August 7; Bolívar's birthday and Battle of Lago de Maracaibo, July 24; La Asunción (Assumption), August 15;* Civil Servants' Day, September 4; Día de la Raza (Columbus Day), October 12; Todos Santos (All Saints' Day), November 1;* Independence of Cartagena City, November 11;* La Inmaculada Concepción (Immaculate Conception), December 8; and Navidad (Christmas Day), December 25. Note: * Movable holidays; when they do not fall on a Monday, these holidays are observed the following Monday.

Flag:
Three equal horizontal bands of yellow, blue, and red, with the coat of arms on the hoist side of the yellow band and an arc of seven white, five-pointed stars centered in the blue band.

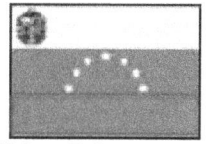

Click to Enlarge Image

1

HISTORICAL BACKGROUND

Early History: On his third voyage to the New World in 1498, Christopher Columbus discovered Venezuela, which Alonso de Ojeda and Amerigo Vespucci explored the next year. The early explorers named the country "Venezuela" (Spanish for little Venice) because they found inhabitants living in stilt houses in lakes. Venezuela's original inhabitants were the Carib and Arawak Amerindian peoples. Spanish explorers founded the settlements of Valencia in 1555 and Santiago de León de Caracas in 1567. Colonial Venezuela's primary value to Spain was geographic. During its annual journey between Portobelo, in present-day Panama, and Cuba, the Spanish bullion fleet depended on Venezuela's long Caribbean coastline for security from foreign enemies and pirates. For the first two and a half centuries of colonial rule, Venezuela lacked political unity, in part because it was of no economic importance to Spanish officials.

By the late sixteenth century, agriculture had become Venezuela's chief economic activity. The colonial economy became centralized around the city of Caracas as a result of developments such as the growth of the cocoa trade, the Spanish crown's granting in 1728 of exclusive trading rights in Venezuela to the Basque-run Caracas Company, and Spain's suppression of the 1749 revolt. In recognition of this growth, Caracas was given political-military authority as the seat of the Captaincy General of Venezuela in 1777, marking the first instance of recognition of Venezuela as a political entity. Nine years later, its designation was changed to the Audiencia de Venezuela, thus granting Venezuela judicial and administrative authority as well.

Independence: Periods of political instability, dictatorial rule, and revolutionary turbulence characterized much of Venezuela's nineteenth-century history. In the first decade, after almost three centuries on the periphery of the Spanish American empire, Venezuela found itself at the center of the independence movement sweeping Latin America. Led initially by Francisco de Miranda, the best known of the precursors of the Spanish American revolution, the colony rebelled against Spain in 1810. However, the rebellion collapsed as a result of a combination of factors, including local and personal rivalries encountered by Miranda; an earthquake that almost completely destroyed Caracas and other key cities on March 26, 1812; and Miranda's subsequent arrest and death in a Spanish jail. Simón Bolívar Palacios, Venezuela's national hero, native son, and later president, assumed leadership of the struggle for independence. After his victory at Carabobo, Bolívar made a triumphal entry into Caracas in June 1821. Venezuela joined with what are now Colombia, Panama, and Ecuador to form the short-lived República de Gran Colombia (Republic of Greater Colombia), but withdrew in 1830 and became a sovereign state.

Caudillo Rule: After Bolívar's death in December 1830, civilian and military leaders called for the restoration of legitimate authority. The century of the caudillo (or caudillismo, the system of rule by a strongman who exercises dictatorial powers), featuring a series of changes in power from one commander to another, started auspiciously with 16 relatively peaceful and prosperous years under the authority of General Juan Aguerrevere (José Antonio) Páez (president, 1830–31, 1837, 1838–43, 1846–47, 1861–63) and several other caudillos. Regarded as second only to Bolívar as a national hero, Páez was twice elected president under the 1830 constitution. A mestizo, he established the pattern of dictatorial rule, ruling with the support of the criollo elite as long as coffee prices remained high. In the 1840s, coffee prices plunged, and the elite divided into two factions: those who remained with Páez called themselves Conservatives, and his rivals called themselves Liberals. Between 1858 and 1863, local caudillos engaged in a chaotic power struggle known as the Federal War because the Liberals favored federalism. In 1870 Antonio Guzmán Blanco (president, 1870–77, 1879–84, 1886–87) finally restored central government authority and ruled for 18 years.

For most of the first half of the twentieth century, until 1958, a series of military dictators who promoted the oil industry and allowed for some social reforms ruled Venezuela. During the regime of General Juan Vicente Gómez (president, 1908–10, 1922–29, 1931–35), oil was discovered in the Maracaibo Basin, and Venezuela changed from a poor, largely agrarian country into one of the richest nations in Latin America. A military coup led by General Marcos Pérez Jiménez (president, 1952–58) overthrew President Rómulo Gallegos Freire, Venezuela's first democratically elected president, on November 24, 1948, after only 10 months in office, ending a brief three-year experiment in democracy known as the *trienio*, or triennium (1945–48).

The Restoration of Democracy: In 1958 a coalition of political groups ousted Pérez Jiménez and restored democracy. Historians have often pointed to the second inauguration of Rómulo Betancourt (president, 1945–48, 1959–64) as the pivotal point in four centuries of Venezuelan history. After nearly a century and a half as perhaps the most extreme example of Latin America's post-independence affliction of caudillismo and military rule, the event, augmented with the adoption of a new constitution in 1961, clearly marked a new era for the country. Venezuela's political life since 1959 has been defined by uninterrupted civilian constitutional rule. After becoming the first president to have served a full term of office, Betancourt was succeeded in 1964 by Raúl Leoni (president, 1964–69) and in 1969 by Rafael Caldera Rodríguez (president, 1969–74). Caldera Rodríguez did much to create economic and political stability, although the latter was marred by terrorist abductions and assassinations. Stability increased in 1974, after the election of Carlos Andrés Pérez (president, 1974–79, 1989–93) of the Democratic Action Party (Acción Democrática—AD). However, Pérez's first term coincided with a fourfold rise in oil prices in late 1973, and by 1979 the Venezuelan economy had stalled and corruption was widespread. At the end of 1989, the so-called Caracazo riots, in which more than 200 people were killed, was a response to an economic austerity program launched by then-President Pérez. In February 1992, a group of army lieutenant colonels led by Lieutenant Colonel Hugo Chávez Frías, an outspoken paratroop commander, mounted an unsuccessful coup attempt, claiming that the events of 1989 showed that the political system no longer served the interests of the people. A year later, Congress impeached Pérez on corruption charges. In 1994 public disaffection with the political system compelled President Rafael Caldera (president, 1969–74, 1994–98) to pardon Chávez, who had attained folk-hero status while in prison.

The Chávez Presidency: Until the elections of December 1998, the president had always been a representative of one of the two so-called traditional parties—the AD, which is social democratic; and the Social Christian Party (Comité de Organización Política Electoral Independiente—COPEI), which is Christian Democratic. However, by 1998 the AD and COPEI had become largely discredited because of their association with corrupt and inept governments. Exploiting the popular desire for new leadership, Chávez ran for president in the December 1998 elections as the candidate of Patriotic Pole (Polo Patriótico—PP), an alliance of his own Fifth Republic Movement (Movimiento Quinta República—MVR) and two other leftist parties, Homeland for All (Patria Para Todos—PPT) and Movement Toward Socialism (Movimiento al Socialismo—MAS). He won a landslide victory, garnering more votes than any candidate in

Venezuela's history. Part of his program of radical change was a complete rewriting of the 1961 constitution by a specially elected Constituent Assembly, as approved by a referendum held in April 1999. In a national referendum held in December 1999, 72 percent of the population ratified the new constitution. On July 30, 2000, Chávez was reelected president with 60 percent of the vote for a six-year term.

In 2001 many middle-class Venezuelans became disenchanted with the Chávez government's failure to deliver on promises to improve personal security, create jobs, and generate economic growth. Chávez's flouting of constitutional procedures in favor of cronyism alienated many Venezuelans, including some top military officers who viewed his politically motivated, high-level military promotions as a replacement of professionalism with cronyism. A broad-based opposition front, the Democratic Coordinator (Coordinadora Democrática—CD), with the support of the conservative business chambers, unions, and Venezuelan Petroleum, staged two national strikes in 2002–3. In the first antigovernment protest in March 2002, the military briefly deposed Chávez, but loyal army elements restored him to the presidency two days later. Moreover, the opposition failed to oust Chávez in a national referendum on August 15, 2004. Judged by outside observers as a free and fair vote, the referendum confirmed Chávez's rule until January 2007, when his presidential mandate is scheduled to end. In the absence of a more popular challenger, however, Chávez could be reelected to a second six-year term.

GEOGRAPHY

Click to Enlarge Image

Location: Located in northern South America, Venezuela is bordered to the north by the Caribbean Sea and the North Atlantic Ocean, to the east by Guyana, to the south by Brazil, and to the west by Colombia.

Size: Venezuela has a total area of 912,050 square kilometers (land: 882,050 square kilometers; water: 30,000 square kilometers), or more than twice the size of California.

Land Boundaries: Venezuela's borders total 4,993 kilometers, of which 2,200 kilometers adjoin Brazil; 2,050 kilometers, Colombia; and 743 kilometers, Guyana.

Disputed Territory: Venezuela has territorial disputes with both its western and eastern South American neighbors. Colombia and Venezuela dispute substantial maritime territory lying off the Guajira Peninsula and in the Golfo de Venezuela (Gulf of Venezuela). Although this dispute is being resolved through bilateral negotiations, elements of national prestige have made it a national issue in both countries in recent decades. Venezuela claims two-thirds of Guyana, or all of the 146,000-square-kilometer area lying west of the Essequibo, Guyana's longest river, which runs north to the Atlantic Ocean and provides a natural dividing line through the small, English-speaking enclave. This claim precludes any discussion of a maritime boundary with Guyana. In October 1999, in response to Guyana's granting of oil and mineral contracts to foreign companies to operate in the Essequibo region, Venezuela's legislature voided the 1899 Tribunal of Arbitration Treaty that determined boundaries between the two countries.

Venezuela also has a territorial dispute with Dominica and its Eastern Caribbean neighbors—Saint Kitts and Nevis, Saint Lucia, and Saint Vincent and the Grenadines—over Aves (Bird) Island, which is located 568 kilometers north of Venezuela and 113 kilometers west of Dominica. France, the Netherlands, and the United States recognize Venezuela's claim that the 0.35-square-kilometer isle sustains human habitation and therefore creates a Venezuelan exclusive economic zone/continental shelf extending over a large portion of the Caribbean Sea.

Length of Coastline: Venezuela's coastline totals 2,800 kilometers.

Maritime Claims: Venezuela claims a 200-nautical mile exclusive economic zone, a 12-nautical mile territorial sea, a 15-nautical mile contiguous zone, and jurisdiction over the continental shelf to a 200-meter depth or to the depth of resource exploitation.

Topography: The Orinoco and various mountain ranges divide the country into four distinct regions, with different climates: the dry, windless, and hot Maracaibo Lowlands in the far northwest; the northwestern Andean mountains and highlands stretching from southwest of the Maracaibo Basin across Northern Venezuela and including Pico Bolívar (La Columna), which is the highest point at 5,007 meters above sea level; the vast central Orinoco plains (llanos), located between the Merida Range and the Orinoco to the south and covering one-third of the country, much of it less than 50 meters in elevation; and the tropical Guiana Highlands in the southeast, with elevations of up to 3,500 meters. The world's highest waterfall, Angel Falls, is located in Venezuela's Guiana Highlands, which comprise more than half of the area of the country. The wild and largely unexplored Guiana Highlands are rich in mineral resources and in developed and undeveloped hydroelectric power.

Principal Rivers: The Orinoco is by far the most important of the more than 1,000 rivers in the country. At between 2,140 and 2,500 kilometers, the Orinoco is the third-longest river in South America, after the Paraná (4,000 to 4,700 kilometers) and the Amazon (6,296 to 6,516 kilometers). The Orinoco originates in Venezuela's remote southern Amazonas territory, at an elevation of 1,074 meters, and receives more than 2,000 tributaries—including the Apure, Arauca, Caroní, Caura, Guaviare, Meta, and Ventuari—during its northeastern course to the Atlantic, creating the Orinoco Delta region. The Orinoco has the third-largest drainage basin (1,086 square kilometers) in South America and, at 28,000 cubic meters per second, the fourth-highest water discharge in the world (after the Amazon's 180,000; the Congo's 42,000; and the Yangtze's 35,000). Downstream from its headwaters, the Orinoco divides in two; one-third of its flow passes through the Brazo Casiquiare (Casiquiare Channel) into a tributary of the Amazon, and the remainder passes into the main Orinoco channel. Most of the rivers rising in the northern mountains flow southeastward to the Apure, which crosses the llanos in a generally eastward direction. The fast-flowing Caroní originates in the Guiana Highlands and flows northward into the Orinoco upstream from Ciudad Guyana.

Climate: Located entirely within the tropics, Venezuela has a climate that is tropical, hot, and humid. The country has two distinct seasons: rainy (June–October) and dry (November–May). The rainy season is called *invierno* (winter), and the dry season, *verano* (summer). The wettest months are August–October, with an average rainfall of 145 millimeters; the driest months are January–April, with an average rainfall of 8 millimeters. The hottest months are May–

September, averaging 18° C to 32° C; the coldest month is January, averaging 2° C to 13° C. However, temperatures vary according to elevation. Coastal and lowland areas are hot year-round; the highlands have a more moderate climate. With an elevation of about 1,000 meters above sea level, Caracas, situated in the Ávila Mountains, has an average temperature of 22° C, with little seasonal variation, but daytime highs can reach about 32° C.

Natural Resources: Venezuela's hydropower and mineral resources, including bauxite, coal, diamonds, gold, iron ore, natural gas, and petroleum, are vast. Its huge oil reserves, the largest in South America and the sixth largest in the world, ensure that the country will remain a major oil producer for at least the next 100 years. Venezuela has billions of barrels of extra-heavy crude oil and bitumen deposits, most of which are situated in the Orinoco Belt, located in Central Venezuela (estimates of recoverable reserves range from 100 to 270 billion barrels). The country's largely untapped natural gas reserves, totaling 148 trillion cubic feet, are the second largest in the Western Hemisphere (behind the United States) and the eighth largest in the world. Venezuela also has vast forest reserves, although they are dwindling rapidly as a result of the constant expansion of cattle-grazing land.

Land Use: Arable land constitutes 2.95 percent of the country's area; permanent crops, 0.92 percent; and other, 96.13 percent. In 1998 an estimated total of 540 square kilometers were irrigated; 16.5 percent of cropland was irrigated in 1999. Approximately 10 million hectares of forest have been allocated for timber production.

Environmental Factors: Venezuela is subject to earthquakes, floods, rockslides, mudslides, and periodic droughts. It ranks among the top 10 of the world's most ecologically diverse countries. However, it has suffered great environmental degradation. Venezuela has the third-highest deforestation rate in South America at 1.1 percent. The Guri dam, one of the world's largest, flooded a massive forested area and is now being filled with silt deposited by runoff from deforested areas. Environmental issues include sewage pollution into Lago de Valencia, located not far to the west of Caracas; oil and urban pollution of Lago de Maracaibo, located in northwestern Zulia State; deforestation; soil degradation; and urban and industrial pollution, especially along the Caribbean coast. Current concerns also include irresponsible mining operations that endanger the rain-forest ecosystem and indigenous peoples. Successive governments have attempted to develop environmental regulations. However, only 35 percent to 40 percent of Venezuela's land is regulated thus far, 29 percent as part of about 100 national parks.

Time Zone: Venezuela Standard Time is four hours behind Greenwich Mean Time (GMT–4).

SOCIETY

Population: In mid-2004 Venezuela's estimated population totaled 26.2 million; the estimated population growth rate was 1.9 percent; and the population was projected to reach 35.3 million in 2025 and 41.7 million in 2050. The last five-year national census was conducted in 2001, when the population was estimated at 23.2 million. Venezuela's population density is low. The country had 25.5 people per square kilometer in 2004, with 93 percent of the population living in urban centers and 7 percent in rural areas. Population density is greatest near the coast, the area with the lowest rainfall average in the country and the most available transportation routes; it is lowest in the south. In July 2004, Venezuela's net migration rate was an estimated –0.04 migrant(s) per 1,000 population.

Demography: According to 2004 estimates, the country's demographic profile was as follows: the age category of 0 to 14 years constituted 30.5 percent of the population (male 3,930,413; female 3,687,744); 15 to 64 years, 64.5 percent (male 8,107,382; female 8,034,905); and 65 years and older, 5 percent (male 571,289; female 685,654). The 2001 census figures varied only slightly from these estimates: 0 to 14 years: 33.1 percent; 15 to 64 years, 62.0 percent; and 65 years and older, 4.9 percent. Also according to 2004 estimates, the sex ratio at birth was 1.08 male(s) per female; less than 15 years of age, 1.07 male(s) per female; 15 to 64 years, 1.01 male(s) per female; 65 years and older, 0.83 male(s) per female; and the total population, 1.02 male(s) per females. The total median age was 25.2 years (male: 24.6; female: 25.8). The total fertility rate was 2.3 children born per woman, and the birthrate was 24 births per 1,000 population. Infant mortality totaled 23 deaths per 1,000 live births (26.2 deaths per 1,000 live births for males and 19.6 deaths per 1,000 live births for females). The death rate was an estimated 4.9 deaths per 1,000 population. Life expectancy at birth for the total population was 74.1 years (male, 71.0 years; female, 77.3 years).

Ethnic Groups and Languages: Venezuela's population includes inhabitants of Spanish, Italian, Portuguese, Arab, German, and African ancestry, as well as indigenous peoples. Although not classified by the 2001 census, an estimated 67 percent of the population is mestizo (mixed race); 21 percent, Caucasian; 10 percent, black; and 2 percent, indigenous. Venezuela's largest expatriate community (a minimum of 1.6 million) consists of Colombians. In 2004 estimates of the number of Colombians residing in Venezuela were as high as 4 million, of whom more than three-fourths were illegal. About 200,000 Amerindians in the remote interior speak Indian dialects. Spanish is the official language.

Religion: For centuries, Roman Catholicism was the country's official religion. The percentage of Venezuelans who are still nominally Roman Catholic is estimated to be as high as 96, with the remaining 4 percent belonging to various Protestant denominations (2 percent) or other religions (2 percent). However, the official Venezuelan government Web site puts the figure at 92 percent, with 8 percent belonging to other religions.

Education and Literacy: Of Venezuelans age 15 and older, 93.4 percent can read and write, one of the highest literacy rates in the region. The literacy rate in 2003 was estimated to be 93.8 percent for males and 93.1 percent for females. Although the Venezuelan education system is overextended and underfunded, the Venezuelan government remains committed to the idea that every citizen is entitled to a free education. Nine years of education are compulsory. The school year extends from February until November. The student population and the education budget have increased, but many children do not attend school because they are undocumented aliens or because of poverty. An estimated 20 percent of the population is without any formal education. The Ministry of Education's efforts are aimed at adapting the curriculum to the demands of an increasingly technological society, expanding compulsory education, and upgrading teacher qualifications.

Venezuela has more than 90 institutions of higher education, with more than 6 million students. Higher education remains free under the 1999 constitution and was receiving 35 percent of the education budget, even though it accounted for only 11 percent of the student population. More than 70 percent of higher-education students come from the wealthiest quintile of the population. In 2003 the Chávez government withheld funding from the country's universities in an alleged attempt, according to rectors of those institutions, to punish them. (All of the major public university rectors were elected on antigovernment platforms.) In July 2003, the government established the Bolivarian University while withholding budgeted funds to many of the existing universities.

Health: Extensive inoculation programs and the availability of low- or no-cost health care provided by the Venezuelan Institute of Social Security have made Venezuela's health care infrastructure one of the more advanced in Latin America. Once the most comprehensive and well funded in the region, the health care system has deteriorated sharply since the 1980s. Government expenditures on health care constituted an estimated 4.1 percent of gross domestic product in 2002. Total health expenditures per capita in 2001 totaled US$386. Per capita government expenditures on health in 2001 totaled US$240. State hospitals are inefficient, crowded, underfunded, and poorly maintained. Private hospitals and clinics and the qualifications of their medical personnel are comparable to U.S. standards. Private health services are costly and largely unregulated.

During the 1995–99 period, the mortality rate by broad groups of causes per 100,000 population was 162.3 for diseases of the circulatory system, 63.8 for malignant neoplasms, 55.3 for external causes, 53.6 for communicable diseases, and 22.4 for certain conditions originating before birth. Several transmissible diseases, including dengue fever, malaria, measles, and tuberculosis, have reappeared in recent years. In August 2001, President Chávez announced a national campaign to fight the dengue fever epidemic that had infected 24,000 and killed four. Child immunization for measles in 2002 (as a percentage of under 12 months) was 78 percent, as compared with 84 percent in 1999. In 1999 an estimated 62,000 Venezuelans were living with acquired immune deficiency syndrome (AIDS); and in 2001 an estimated 2,000 people died from AIDS. At the end of 2003, the percentage of the population between the ages of 15 to 49 with human immunodeficiency virus (HIV)/AIDS was 0.7. In 2000, 85 percent of the urban population and 70 percent of the rural population had access to improved water. Improved sanitation was available to 71 percent of the urban population and 48 percent of the rural population.

Welfare: Although Venezuela's mandatory public social security system is designed to provide retirement, survivorship, and disability benefits, these benefits are meager as a result of widespread corruption, mismanagement, and the country's poor economic performance. Many retirement "savings funds" are managed by the major banks or by private companies. Venezuelan Petroleum and the armed forces run the largest non-bank-managed pension funds. President Chávez's three main "social justice" objectives are to guarantee social rights in a universal and equitable way, improve the distribution of income and wealth, and strengthen social participation and generate citizen power in public decision-making.

In late 2003, President Chávez committed his government to funding US$1 billion in new social programs. High oil prices throughout 2004 aided funding for this expansion. Serious social problems include widespread poverty, income inequality, and criminal violence. As inequality has worsened, the poor have suffered disproportionately. In 2003–4, 86 percent of the population was living in general poverty, as compared with 1989, when 66.5 percent of the population was living in poverty and 29.6 percent in extreme poverty. These high rates result primarily from lower real wages earned by employees and high rates of unemployment and underemployment. Violence and discrimination against women, abuse of children, discrimination against people with disabilities, and inadequate protection of the rights of indigenous people also are problems. Child labor has increased as economic conditions have worsened. Trafficking in persons also is a problem, although the government has taken steps to reduce corruption among immigration authorities.

ECONOMY

Overview: Petroleum has been the mainstay of the Venezuelan economy since the 1920s and accounts for between one-quarter and one-third of gross domestic product (GDP), about 80 percent of export earnings, and as much as one-half of the central government's operating revenue. Venezuelan Petroleum is one of the world's largest oil companies and Venezuela's leading employer, although it fired 18,000 of its 48,000 employees after the strike of 2002–3. The company's revenues in 2004 were an estimated US$32 billion. Venezuela was the world's fifth largest oil producer until the end of the 1990s, when it was overtaken by Mexico. Since the government reopened the oil sector to private capital in the 1990s and modified oil taxation, the government's share of oil revenue from Venezuelan Petroleum has been falling and amounted to only US$0.39 per US$1 by 2000, as compared with US$0.71 per US$1 in 1981. Dependence on oil-export revenue makes Venezuela particularly vulnerable to fluctuations in the global economy. Although Venezuela benefited from the increase in petroleum prices beginning in the early 1970s, it suffered from oil price declines in 1986, 1998, and 2001. Oil prices started to recover again in March 2002. Despite a massive windfall in oil revenue resulting from rising world prices since late 2002, Venezuela has been running a sizable central government deficit, largely as a result of fiscal profligacy.

After Hugo Chávez was reelected president in July 2000, capital flight escalated and has intensified since then as political tensions have increased. Domestic political instability culminated in a disastrous two-month national oil strike from December 2002 to February 2003, temporarily halting economic activity and leading to an unprecedented collapse of GDP in 2002–3. However, the economy, aided by high oil prices, recovered in 2004.

Gross Domestic Product (GDP): Average real incomes fell sharply as a result of GDP growth averaging only 1 percent per year during the 1985–2003 period. The two-month general strike that began in December 2002 was a key factor in the collapse of real GDP in 2002 (–8.9 percent) and 2003 (–9.2 percent). Total GDP in 2002 was only US$95.4 billion, as compared with US$126.2 billion in 2001. In 2004, with the surge in oil prices, the economy rebounded from the crisis of 2002–3. Venezuela's GDP grew by 17.3 percent in 2004 to US$109 billion, with the oil sector growing by 8.7 percent and non-oil activities up 17.8 percent. According to the Central Bank, the recovery in the GDP in 2004 also resulted from an increase in the demand for consumer goods and an increase in investment, along with declining inflation, unemployment, and interest rates. Real GDP growth is expected to reach 5 percent in 2005 but slow to 3.5 percent in 2006. GDP composition by sector in 2004 was estimated as follows: agriculture, 5 percent; industry, 50 percent; and services, 45 percent. The informal sector has grown rapidly since 1989.

Government Budget: Since 1999 the Chávez government's public financing has been aided by increases in the price of petroleum. Nevertheless, greatly increased oil revenues have been offset by sizable increases in public spending. Budget revenues in 2004 totaled an estimated US$19.3 billion, and expenditures an estimated US$24.3 billion, including capital expenditures of US$2.6 billion. With increased oil and non-oil revenue, the government intends to reduce its deficit from an estimated 4.3 percent of gross domestic product (GDP) in 2003 and 3.3 percent of GDP in 2004 to 2.8 percent of GDP in 2005 and 0.6 percent of GDP in 2007. The total public debt constituted an estimated 38.8 percent of GDP in 2004, as compared with 27.8 percent of GDP in 1999. In March 2003, the Venezuelan Workers Confederation, which is the main trade union entity, estimated the public-sector labor debts (unpaid government liabilities owed to active and retired public-sector workers) at US$11 billion.

Inflation: Historically, inflation in Venezuela was low, averaging below 3 percent during 1958–73. However, since the bolívar was floated in February 2002, persistently high rates of inflation have been a problem. The inflation rate (consumer prices) in 2004 was 21.7 percent, down from 27.1 percent in 2003; it is projected to be 19.4 percent in 2005 and 18.7 percent in 2006.

Agriculture: Prior to the 1950s and the initiation of large-scale oil exports, agriculture, fishing, and forestry were central to the Venezuelan economy, producing more than half the gross domestic product (GDP). As the petrochemical industry expanded rapidly in the 1970s and 1980s, however, the proportion of the labor force in agriculture dropped from one-fifth to about one-tenth. Agriculture has continued to decline, accounting for about 5 percent of GDP and 10 percent of employment in 2004. Gross agricultural production growth declined 0.3 percent in 2003 but is estimated to grow by 3 percent in 2004 and 0.5 percent in 2005. The country imports most of its food, mainly from Colombia and the United States. Agricultural products include bananas, beef, coffee, corn, eggs, fish, milk, pork, rice, sorghum, sugarcane, and vegetables.

Venezuela's present-day agriculture is characterized by inefficiency and low investment, with 70 percent of agricultural land owned by 3 percent of agricultural proprietors (one of the highest levels of land concentration in Latin America). According to the Land and Agricultural Reform Law of 2001, public and private land deemed to be illegally held or unproductive is to be redistributed. In December 2004, the government announced plans to accelerate the law's application.

Forestry: Timber from natural forests makes the greatest economic contribution to forest production, constituting more than 90 percent since 1993. The country's area of natural forests is shrinking at an average annual rate of 218,000 hectares, largely as a result of cutting to provide pasturage for cattle. Approximately 10 million hectares of forest have been allocated for timber production. Timber extraction in Venezuela is under government control. In 2001, 14 concession-holding companies were active, carrying out forest-management plans on 1,206,000 hectares. Firewood, mainly for household use and to a lesser extent for cottage industries, represents 50 percent of total wood consumption in Venezuela. Little information is available on the production and use of other forest products. Venezuela's total annual timber consumption is approximately 525,000 cubic meters, 90 percent of it from domestic sources. The sawmill industry included 300 mills in 2001, mostly small and medium-sized.

Fishing: The fishing industry has expanded rapidly since the 1990s. In 2000 the fishing fleet consisted of approximately 15,000 vessels, 94 percent of which were directed to the small-scale artisanal fisheries, 2 percent to mid-water fisheries, and 4 percent to the deep-sea industrial fisheries. The tuna fleet consisted of 31 purse seiners with a transport capacity of greater than 900 tons; 25 operated in the East Pacific ocean. The small-scale fishing fleet consisted of about 16,300 vessels, of which 64 percent operated in the coastal zone and 36 percent in river bays. The mid-water fleet consisted of about 400 shrimp trawlers and 260 vessels for capturing snappers and dusky groupers. The deep-sea fleet had 230 vessels. In 1998 the by-catches production totaled 515,917 tons, of which 89 percent were marine species and 9 percent, river species; exports totaled approximately 120,189 tons.

Mining and Minerals: Venezuela is a major producer and exporter of minerals, notably bauxite, coal, gold, iron ore, and oil, and the state controls most of the country's vast mineral reserves. In 2003 estimated reserves of bauxite totaled 5.2 million tons. The third largest producer of coal in Latin America, after Colombia and Brazil, Venezuela produced 5.8 million short tons (1 short ton=2,000 pounds) in 2002, as compared with 9.3 million short tons in 2000, and exported most of it to other countries in the region, the eastern United States, and Europe. Known reserves for coal total 10.2 billion tons, of which approximately 528 million short tons are recoverable bituminous coal. The main coalfields are located in the western state of Zulia, on the border with Colombia. Other known reserves include natural bitumen (42 billion tons). Exploitable gold reserves, located mostly in the southeast, total an estimated 10,000 tons. In 2003 production totaled 20 million grams (or 20 tons), including 6 million grams attributed to unofficial mining activities, marking a sharp increase from 1999, when only 5.9 million grams were produced. In 2003 Venezuela's estimated reserves of iron ore totaled 14.6 million tons. Proven reserves total 4.1 billion tons, of which 1.7 billion tons are high-grade. Production has been increasing and totaled a record 19.2 million tons in 2003, two-thirds of which were exported. Iron-ore reserves are concentrated in the southeast.

With 77.8 billion barrels of proven oil reserves in 2004, Venezuela has the largest proven oil reserves in South America and the sixth largest in the world—more than Canada, Mexico, and the United States combined. Venezuela's 2002 production of 2.8 million barrels per day (bbl/d) of crude was a drop of 8.3 percent over 2001 and the country's lowest production figure since 1994. In 2003, a year in which production was halted for a couple of months by a general strike and further disrupted by the firing of nearly half of the state oil company's work force, Venezuela's total oil production was an estimated 2.6 million bbl/d. In 2004 oil production totaled about 3 million bbl/d, according to the government's estimate. Prior to President Chávez's December 1998 election, Venezuela regularly exceeded its Organization of the Petroleum Exporting Countries (OPEC)-agreed oil production targets. Chávez has maintained a policy of strict adherence to OPEC quotas and has played a leading role in shifting OPEC from a volume-oriented strategy to one of controlling prices. With planned investments of US$26 billion in oil and natural gas exploration and production between 2004 and 2009, Venezuelan Petroleum expects oil production to reach 5 million bbl/d by 2009.

Industry and Manufacturing: The manufacturing sector is dominated by small- and medium-sized industries oriented toward consumer goods and the domestic market. Industries include petroleum, iron ore mining, construction materials, food processing, textiles, steel, aluminum, and motor vehicle assembly. Manufacturing gross domestic product (GDP) increased by 2.1 percent in 2000, but declined by 8 percent in 2001. Since the late 1990s, the construction industry has been depressed, and its output at the end of 2003 was less than half its level of 1993. The industrial production growth rate in 2004 was an estimated –15.4 percent.

Energy: According to official Venezuelan estimates, oil production in 2004 totaled 3.2 million barrels per day (bbl/d), as compared with 2.6 million bbl/d in 2003. However, independent estimates put the 2004 figure at around 2.6 million bbl/d. According to the Organization of the Petroleum Exporting Countries (OPEC), Venezuelan production, including conventional crude and the upgraded, extra-heavy oil called Syncrude (for synthetic crude), totaled 2.7 million bbl/d as of December 2004. Four joint-venture projects at the José refinery complex on Venezuela's northern coast are converting the extra-heavy crude from approximately 9° API (American Petroleum Institute) crude to lighter Syncrude. Oil consumption in 2003 was between 350,000 and 400,000 bbl/d. Proven oil reserves totaled 77.8 billion barrels in 2004. Untapped natural gas reserves total 148 trillion cubic feet, according to one estimate, or 4.202 trillion cubic meters, according to another. The country's estimated 31.7 billion cubic meters of natural gas production in 2001 was all consumed domestically (60 percent by the oil industry, 11 percent for power generation, 6 percent in petrochemical production, and the remainder by industrial or commercial customers in large cities). However, legislation passed in 1999 opened the natural gas sector to foreign participants, and Venezuela plans to begin exporting liquefied natural gas by 2008.

With 90.3 percent of its population on the national grid, Venezuela has the highest level of electricity provision in Latin America. Venezuelans also consume the most electricity per head in South America, with the help of state subsidies that keep prices low. Electricity consumption in 2001 totaled 81.47 billion kWh. Electricity production in 2001 totaled 87.6 billion kWh. The Raúl Leoni Dam, which is part of the Guri hydroelectric complex, the second or third largest hydroelectric plant in the world, provides about 68 percent of Venezuela's electric power. Smaller plants on the Caroní provide most of the remainder. Despite Venezuela's highly developed hydropower resources, electric-power facilities have strained in recent years to keep up with burgeoning demand for electricity. Aggravating this problem is an estimated 26 percent of electricity consumption that is lost through theft, especially from state-owned generators operating in rural and semi-rural areas.

Services: The services sector accounted for 45 percent of gross domestic product (GDP) and 64 percent of labor in 2004. Financial services contributed 26 percent of GDP in 2003, with eight banks accounting for 73 percent of total assets. The country's 52 banks serve primarily the domestic market.

Despite the country's abundant natural attractions, including the world's highest waterfall, South America's largest lake, and many national parks, the tourism industry remains undeveloped, with the exception of Margarita Island, which is visited by 90 percent of tourists to Venezuela. Poor-quality services and political instability in the country have been disincentives for tourists. The hotel industry suffered a sharp drop in occupancy rates in 2002–3. Nevertheless, with its tropical climate and diverse landscape Venezuela has become a popular destination for visitors from Belgium, Britain, Canada, Germany, and Holland. As a result, the numbers of tour operators and travel agents within the country are increasing rapidly. An estimated 12,000 U.S. tourists visit Venezuela annually.

Labor: The labor force totaled an estimated 11.4 million workers in 2004. The labor force by occupation in 1997 was estimated as follows: agriculture, 13 percent; industry, 23 percent; and services, 64 percent. Updated figures were unavailable in early 2005, with the exception of agriculture, which declined to 10 percent in 2003. The unemployment rate in 2004 fell to 10.9 percent, as compared with 14.9 percent in 1999. Employment in the informal sector has grown rapidly during the Chávez years, but may be slowing down. The informal economy employed 51.2 percent of the labor force in 2002, 52.4 percent in 2003, and only 48.7 percent in 2004.

Foreign Economic Relations: The United States traditionally has been Venezuela's principal market for oil exports and the main supplier of imports. In 2002 the United States absorbed 59 percent of Venezuela's exports and supplied 41 percent of its imports. In 2003 the United States supplied only about one-third of Venezuela's imports. Nevertheless, Venezuela remains the United States' third-largest export market in Latin America, purchasing U.S. machinery, transportation equipment, agricultural commodities, and auto parts. In 2003 up to two-thirds of Venezuelan exports went to the United States. As much as 60 percent of Venezuela's crude oil exports go to the United States, not including other petroleum refined in the Caribbean before being shipped to the United States. Venezuela's share of U.S. imports of petroleum has been decreasing since 1997; actual imports from Venezuela have declined from 1.8 million bbl/d to about 1.5 million bbl/d. In 2004 Venezuela was the fourth largest supplier of crude oil to the United States. Nevertheless, Venezuela's importance to the U.S. oil supply and Venezuela's oil export revenues are likely to remain of paramount importance to both countries.

Other export partners in 2003 included the Netherlands Antilles, the European Union (EU), Brazil, the Dominican Republic, Colombia, Canada, and Cuba. Other import sources in 2003 included the EU, Colombia, Brazil, and Mexico. Trade between Brazil and Venezuela doubled to US$1.6 billion in 2004 from 2003 and was expected to reach US$3 billion in 2005. President Chávez's protectionist policies and foreign-exchange controls reduced bilateral commerce with Colombia by nearly 50 percent in 2002–3. After Venezuela relaxed its trade restrictions in the second half of 2004, Colombian exports to Venezuela jumped, and bilateral trade between the two neighbors exceeded US$2 billion in 2004. However, in response to the capture in Caracas of a Colombian guerrilla leader by agents of Colombia's government in December 2004, Venezuela suspended commercial links with Colombia on January 15, 2005.

The Chávez government's trade policy is to reduce Venezuela's commercial dependence on the United States by expanding its trade relations with China and Russia and diversifying the country's trading partners. It also has signed bilateral accords with Iran and Cuba. As a result of an oil-supply agreement, Venezuela became Cuba's main trading partner in 2000. Since October 2000, Cuba has received 53,000 barrels per day of oil and derivatives from Venezuela on easy, long-term credit terms, with the exception of a five-month period following the April 2002 coup attempt, when this arrangement was suspended. In December 2004, President Chávez visited Cuba and signed a series of agreements covering trade and Venezuelan investment rights in Cuba, energy, education, and medical cooperation.

The Chávez government also has maintained a critical stance toward the proposed Free Trade Area of the Americas and has promoted instead a "Bolivarian" alternative model of integration that excludes the United States. Venezuela has partial free-trade agreements with Chile, countries of Central America, and the Caribbean Economic Community (Caricom). Despite President Chávez's anti-U.S. government rhetoric and his efforts to reduce his country's trade dependence on the United States, U.S.-Venezuelan commercial ties remain close, and the United States is expected to remain Venezuela's dominant trading partner for the foreseeable future.

Imports: Imports of goods free on board (f.o.b.) totaled US$10.3 billion in 2003, US$17.3 billion in 2004, and a projected US$19.7 billion in 2005. In 2003 the United States accounted for 33.7 percent of Venezuela's imports; the European Community, 21.6 percent (including Italy, 10 percent; and Germany, 7 percent); Japan, 12.8 percent; Colombia, 8.5 percent; Brazil, 6.6 percent; and Mexico, 5.0 percent. Venezuela's total imports by main commodity group in 2003 were agricultural products, 19.3 percent; mining products, 3.6 percent; and manufactures, including machinery, transportation equipment, and semi-manufactured goods, 76.9 percent.

Exports: Exports of goods free on board (f.o.b.) totaled US$26.9 billion in 2003, US$39.4 billion in 2004, and a projected US$41.5 billion in 2005. About 80 percent of the country's export revenue is derived from oil earnings (US$20.8 billion in 2003). Export destinations in 2003 included the United States, 44.3 percent to 67 percent, depending on the source; the Netherlands Antilles, 16.6 percent; the European Union (EU), 12.6 percent; Brazil, 3.7 percent; the Dominican Republic, 3.0 percent; Colombia, 2.6 percent; and Cuba, 2.6 percent. Other than petroleum, the most important exports include agricultural products, aluminum, basic manufactures, bauxite, cement, chemicals, fruit, iron ore, paper products, petrochemicals, plastics, seafood, steel, and tobacco. Of these products, aluminum and steel are particularly important. In 2003 Venezuela's total exports by main commodity group were mining products, 77.0 percent; manufactures, 12.3 percent; and agricultural products, 1.2 percent.

Trade Balance: Venezuela improved its trade balance in 2004 to about US$22 billion, with exports totaling US$39.4 billion and imports, US$17.3 billion.

Balance of Payments: Venezuela's oil revenue often allows the country to run a large surplus on its current-account balance. The current account surplus expanded from US$11.5 billion in 2003 to a record US$14.6 billion in 2004, mainly as a result of high oil prices. As a percentage of gross domestic product (GDP), the current-account balance was 13.5 in 2003, 13.9 in 2004, and an estimated 3.5 in 2005 and 2.5 in 2006. Deficits on the capital and financing account rose sharply in 1999–2004 and totaled US$3.2 billion in 2003 and US$12.7 billion in 2004.

External Debt: The foreign debt totaled an estimated US$32.5 billion in 2004, a figure that generally has been stable in recent years. Reserves of foreign exchange and gold totaled an estimated US$20.7 billion 2004.

Foreign Investment: Foreign direct investment (FDI) has averaged about US$450 million a year since 1992, when it was only US$150 million. In 2000 FDI reached US$4.7 billion but declined to US$3.7 billion in 2001 and US$0.8 billion in 2002, rising to US$1.3 billion in 2003 and 2004. The downturn in Venezuela's FDI in 2002–3 has been attributed to political and financial instability. Venezuela's FDI has been declining in most non-oil sectors since 1998, with the main exception of telecommunications. FDI as a percentage of the gross domestic product (GDP) in 2001 amounted to 2.8 percent. Gross fixed investment in 2004 was an estimated 3.7 percent of GDP. In order to maintain oil revenue, the Chávez government has been focusing its FDI efforts on the country's abundant energy reserves. However, Venezuela's 2001 Hydrocarbons Law, which became effective in January 2002, is expected to discourage foreign investment in the Venezuelan oil industry by raising royalties paid by private companies to between 20 percent and 30 percent, as compared with the previous 1 percent to 16.7 percent. At the same time, the law guarantees the state oil company at least a 51-percent stake in any project regarding exploration, production, transportation, and initial storage of oil. The government's investment laws and regulations also have discouraged most FDI in the non-oil sectors. Moreover, the government intends to review current mining investments in order to strengthen investment commitments and improve the terms of current agreements.

Foreign Aid: Because of its abundant natural resources, Venezuela did not need to turn to foreign aid until it was hit by an economic crisis in 1989. From 1994 to 2002, the European Union (EU) committed €130 million. European aid is focusing on technical and financial co-operation projects in the areas of education, health, prison conditions, regional development, environment, and the fight against drugs. A total of €63.8 million has been earmarked for Venezuela for the period 2000–2006 for technical and financial co-operation and rehabilitation and reconstruction.

Venezuela currently is not receiving any major foreign aid from the United States. In response to heavy rains, landslides and persistent flooding in the north-central region of Venezuela that began on February 7, 2005, the U.S. Agency for International Development's Office of Foreign Disaster Assistance provided US$50,000 through the U.S. Embassy in Caracas to the Venezuelan Red Cross for the purchase and distribution of emergency relief items.

Currency and Exchange Rate: Venezuela's currency is the bolívar (Bs1=100 céntimos). During the July 1996 to January 2002 period, the bolívar moved in a sliding band, and as a result it became increasingly overvalued in real terms. In February 2002, prompted by spiraling capital flight, falling reserves (under US$10 billion), and a deepening fiscal crisis, the government floated the bolívar. In response to continuing rampant capital flight and dwindling international reserves, the government and the Central Bank imposed draconian foreign-exchange controls on January 23, 2003, and created, on February 5, the Currency Administration Commission to administer and implement foreign-exchange controls. The average exchange rate in 2004 was Bs1,891.3=US$1. The official exchange rate was devalued by 10.8 percent in March 2005 to US$1=Bs2,150.0.

Fiscal Year: Calendar year.

TRANSPORTATION AND TELECOMMUNICATIONS

Overview: Venezuela's transportation system is well developed, with the main exception of the railroad system. The transportation density network is higher along the coasts and gets lower toward the center and south of the country. The south of the country is not accessible by land. The road network is the principal means of transport for goods and people and is considered one of the best in Latin America. Buses are the primary form of transport throughout most of Venezuela. They run frequently and are inexpensive but are generally slow and crowded. For long-distance travel, the first-class bus service throughout the country is generally fast and efficient. Various small airlines serve the domestic network, but most operate at a loss and with very old equipment.

Roads: In 2004 Venezuela had approximately 81,000 kilometers of roads, including 31,200 kilometers of paved highways, 24,800 kilometers of gravel-surfaced roads, and 25,000 kilometers of unimproved dirt tracks. The road network includes a section of the Pan-American Highway running from Caracas to Colombia. Roads in Caracas and other large cities are comparable to those in U.S. cities. In rural areas, the road network is less developed than in the cities. Although control over highways devolved to the state governments in 1989, expected improvements in the road infrastructure failed to materialize.

Railroads: The country's very small railroad system, half of which is privately owned, is undeveloped and not a viable alternative to the roads. In 2003 the country had a total of 682 kilometers of standard 1.435-meter gauge railroad. A 3,447-kilometer-long system of local, regional, and national lines is planned for 2020. Caracas has a modern subway system, which was opened in 1982.

Ports and Shipping: Venezuela has 13 major ports and harbors: Amuay, Bajo Grande, El Tablazo, La Guaira, La Salina, Maracaibo, Matanzas, Palua, Puerto Cabello, Puerto la Cruz, Puerto Ordaz, Puerto Sucre, and Punta Cardón. Of these, La Guaira, Puerto Cabello, and Maracaibo handle 80 percent of the cargo. In 2003 the Merchant Marine totaled 48 ships (1,000 GRT or more).

Inland Waterways: Venezuela has 7,100 kilometers of inland waterways. The Orinoco and Lago de Maracaibo are navigable by oceangoing vessels. In 2003 the Orinoco was navigable for 400 kilometers. However, navigability of the Orinoco may be affected by substantial seasonal variations in water levels, with the lowest levels in March and April. Development of the waterway infrastructure, especially along the Orinoco and Apure, is a government priority.

Civil Aviation and Airports: Since its creation in November 2002, a semi-autonomous agency, the National Institute of Civil Aviation (Instituto Nacional de Aviación Civil—INAC), which is attached to the Ministry of Infrastructure, has supervised and regulated civil aviation in Venezuela. Of Venezuela's 431 airfields, about 280 are licensed landing facilities, but only about 30 have regular scheduled traffic. All others are for general aviation, and some are privately owned. The country's main international airport is Maiquetía Simón Bolívar International Airport, which serves Caracas; the only airport that is owned and operated by the federal government, it is run by a semi-autonomous agency attached to the Ministry of Infrastructure.

The other main airport serves the city of Maracaibo. In 2004 Venezuela had an estimated total of 127 paved runways, including 5 more than 3,047 meters long.

In 2003 the financial condition of the airline industry in Venezuela was very poor, and only three airlines were reported to be operating at a profit: Aeropostal-Wings of Venezuela, Santa Barbara Airlines, and Avior. Venezuela's main domestic airline until it went bankrupt in 1999 was Avensa (Venezuelan Airlines); it now operates on a reduced scale. About half a dozen smaller airlines serve as regional carriers. In late 2003, the government announced plans for a new national airline, Conviasa (Venezuelan Consortium of Aeronautical Industries and Air Services), which was awaiting approval by the INAC to begin operating in early 2005.

Pipelines: In 2003 Venezuela's pipelines totaled 992 kilometers for extra-heavy crude; 5,262 kilometers for gas; 7,484 kilometers for oil; 1,681 kilometers for refined products; and 141 kilometers of oil/water line for an unidentified use. The country does not yet have any export pipelines. However, when President Chávez visited Colombia in November 2004, he agreed to build a cross-border oil pipeline for shipping Venezuelan oil to the Pacific coast.

Telecommunications: Since the adoption of a new telecommunications law in June 2000 and privatization of the state telephone company, National Autonomous Telephone Company of Venezuela (CANTV), in November 2000, the sector has been modernized and expanded as a result of a surge of investment. Telephone service in rural areas has been improved substantially, and exchanges and trunk lines increasingly have been digitized. In 2003 the country had almost 3 million telephone subscribers, 112,634 public telephones, and a telephone density of 11.5 per 100 inhabitants. In 2003 Venezuela had 7 million mobile cellular phones in use by 27.3 percent of the population. The mobile phone market is the most competitive and dynamic subsector. Venezuela is linked by a direct dialing network. However, telephone service remains overloaded, and telephoning can be very frustrating, particularly in the larger towns. Smaller towns tend to be better for international calls because there is less competition for lines. Venezuela's domestic satellite system has three earth stations, including one Intelsat (Atlantic Ocean) and one PanAmSat, and is participating with Colombia, Ecuador, Peru, and Bolivia in the construction of an international fiber-optic network. A national inter-urban fiber-optic network capable of digital multimedia services has been installed. Venezuela has three submarine coaxial cables.

In 2003 Venezuela had about 201 AM commercial radio stations, 20 FM radio stations, 11 short-wave stations, and 15 radio stations operated by National Radio of Venezuela, the state broadcasting organization. The country also had 4.1 million televisions, 66 television broadcast stations (plus 45 repeaters), and 5 main television channels. The government owns a national television station, Venezuelan Television; a metropolitan Caracas television station, TV Venezuela; and a newswire service, VenPres, whose directors are named by the president. The number of personal computers per 1,000 of population was 70.9 in 2002. In 2003 the number of Internet hosts totaled 35,301; the number of Internet subscribers totaled 321,330; and the number of Internet users totaled more than 1.5 million, or about 6 percent of the population. Almost 1,000 cybercafés were operating in the country at the end of 2002.

GOVERNMENT AND POLITICS

Government Overview: With the adoption of the country's twenty-seventh constitution on December 15, 1999, Venezuela is a federal republic with a "participative democracy" type of government. The charter provides for direct popular election of the president every six years, with reelection to one consecutive term permissible. Under the new constitution, the traditional three powers of government—executive, legislative, and judicial—have been augmented with two new ones: Citizen Power and Electoral Power.

Executive Branch: The executive branch consists of the president of the republic, who is both chief of state and head of government. Hugo Chávez Frías was elected president on February 3, 1999, with 60 percent of the votes. The president is aided by a vice president and Council of Ministers. The president appoints (and may remove) the vice president. José Vicente Rangel became vice president on April 28, 2002. The president also appoints the members of the Council of Ministers.

Legislative Branch: The legislative branch consists of a unicameral, 165-seat National Assembly (Asamblea Nacional). Its members are elected by popular vote through a combination of proportional representation and direct election to serve five-year terms; three seats are reserved for the indigenous peoples of Venezuela. Members may be reelected up to three times. The National Assembly has the power to name members of the Supreme Tribunal of Justice (Tribuna Suprema de Justicia—TSJ) and Citizen Power (*poder ciudadano*). With a two-thirds vote, the National Assembly may appoint (or abolish) no more than 15 ordinary and special Standing Committees to consider legislation pertaining to particular sectors of national activity. Temporary Committees may be appointed for purposes of research and study. While the assembly is in recess, a Delegated Committee consisting of the president, the vice president, and the presidents of the Standing Committees is in session. Legislation may be introduced by the executive branch; the Delegated Committee, Standing Committees, and members of the National Assembly; and, in their areas of competency, the TSJ, Citizen Power, Electoral Power, and State Legislative Council. The voters (in a number equivalent to at least 0.1 percent of all permanently registered voters) also may propose legislation. Prior to promulgation, an approved law must be sent to the TSJ's Constitutional Division for a ruling on its constitutionality.

As a result of the July 30, 2000, legislative elections, Chávez's pro-government bloc held 108 of the 165 seats, but subsequent party splits reduced the pro-Chávez members to 86 seats. As of early 2005, the seating composition of the National Assembly by party was divided into two main coalitions: the 86-member Parliamentary Bloc for Change (Bloque Parlamentario del Cambio—BPC) and the 79-member Bloc for Parliamentary Autonomy (Bloque por la Autonomía Parlamentaria—BAP). The BPC included President Chávez's Fifth Republic Movement (Movimiento V República—MVR), with 68 seats, and five smaller parties. The BAP included the opposition Democratic Action (Acción Democrática—AD), with 24 seats; and the Social Christian Party (Comité de Organización Política Electoral Independiente—COPEI), with 7 seats, as well as 10 smaller parties.

Judicial Branch: The judicial branch is responsible for administering justice in the name of the republic and by authority of the law. This branch is headed by the Supreme Tribunal of Justice

(Tribuna Suprema de Justicia—TSJ), formerly known as the Supreme Court. In 2004 legislation sponsored by the Chávez administration increased the number of TSJ justices by 12 to 32, thereby giving Chávez near-absolute control of the courts. The National Assembly appoints the justices to serve a single 12-year term. The TSJ exercises control over constitutionality and legality at all levels. The TSJ is divided into plenary, constitutional, political-administrative, electoral, civil, and social and criminal appeals chambers. The TSJ may meet either in the six specialized chambers or in plenary session. The semiautonomous Council of the Judicature, whose members are appointed by the legislative and executive branches, appoints judges and controls the administration of the judiciary. The civilian judiciary is legally independent; however, it is reportedly inefficient and sometimes corrupt, and judges at all levels are subject to influence from a number of sources, including the executive branch.

The judicial branch also includes the lower courts, Public Ministry, Public Defender, penal investigative bodies, employees of the Ministry of Interior and Justice and penitentiary system, and lawyers. The courts are divided geographically into township or parish courts, district or department courts, courts of the first instance, and higher courts. In general, court decisions may be appealed to a higher court, but a case cannot be heard by more than two instances. Only decisions handed down in the second instance by higher courts can be appealed to the TSJ.

Citizen Power: Citizen Power is exercised by the Republican Moral Council (Consejo Moral Republicano), which consists of the ombudsman, the general prosecutor, and the comptroller general of the republic. These officials are responsible for preventing, investigating, and punishing actions perpetrated against the public ethos and administrative morality; guarding the public interest and legal use of the public patrimony; ensuring the application of the principle of legality in all administrative activity of the state; and promoting civic education, solidarity, freedom, democracy, social responsibility, and social work. The National Assembly selects holders of Citizen Power offices for terms of seven years.

Electoral Power: Electoral Power is exercised by the National Electoral Council (Consejo Nacional Electoral—CNE), a new body that replaced the old electoral authorities on adoption of the 1999 constitution. Public confidence in the CNE was shaken by its secretive handling of the August 15, 2004, presidential-recall vote. Entities subordinate to the CNE are the National Electoral Board, the Electoral and Civil Registration Commission, and the Commission of Financial and Political Participation. The CNE regulates electoral laws, proposes the CNE budget, issues directives, nullifies elections in whole or in part, oversees all aspects of elections, organizes elections of syndicates and unions of professionals, oversees electoral and civil registration, organizes the registration of parties, regulates party funding, and guarantees the impartiality and fairness of elections.

Legal System: Venezuela had adopted 23 constitutions since gaining independence from Spain in 1811. The most recent constitution was adopted in 1999 to mark the transition from the Fourth to the Fifth Republic, that is, from a "party-dominated" democracy to "popular" democracy. The country has an open, adversarial court system based on organic laws. It has not accepted compulsory International Court of Justice jurisdiction. The country's criminal legislation is derived from the Penal Code, enacted in 1926 and partially modified in 1964 and 2000. Both civilians and members of the military are tried in civilian courts for committing civil offenses, but the military courts have jurisdiction over civilians who commit military crimes, such as espionage and insurrection.

Administrative Divisions: The Republic of Venezuela is divided into states, the capital district, federal dependencies, and federal territories. The 23 states are Amazonas, Anzoátegui, Apure, Aragua, Barinas, Bolívar, Carabobo, Cojedes, Delta Amacuro, Falcón, Guárico, Lara, Mérida, Miranda, Monagas, Nueva Esparta (consisting of Margarita, Cubagua, and Coche islands), Portuguesa, Sucre, Táchira, Trujillo, Vargas (part of the federal district until 1998), Yaracuy, and Zulia. The states are divided into a total of 156 districts, which are further divided into 613 municipalities. The municipalities are subdivided into parishes. The capital district (formerly called the federal district) includes much of the Caracas metropolitan area and encompasses five municipalities or departments. The 72 federal dependencies include 11 island groups and 311 islands, keys, and islets. The federal territories of Amazonas and Delta Amacuro have the status of a state by special law.

Provincial and Local Government: Venezuelans traditionally have given greater loyalty to their states than to their local government bodies. As a result, local government has not been strong. The powers of the states are restricted to those areas not granted to the nation or the municipalities, and the states remain dependent on the national government for most of their revenue. Each state is headed by a governor, who also serves as the chief agent of the national executive within each state. Governors are elected every three years by universal, direct, and secret ballot. Unicameral state legislative assemblies are popularly elected every three years and exercise limited powers. The states do not have their own judiciary.

Districts are constitutionally independent of the state in economic and administrative matters and subject only to national laws and regulations. Districts are governed by popularly elected councils; elections for council members take place at the same time as those for national officials. Council members serve five-year terms. The number of Council members varies, but all councils are presided over by a chairperson, who serves in that position for a one-year term. The districts are divided into municipalities, which are the primary and autonomous political units within the national organization that are administered in accordance with the principle of local self-government. In each municipality, the government and administration of local interests are in the hands of a mayor, who is elected every three years. Municipal councils, also elected every three years, make policy on local matters and serve as administrative units in charge of garbage collection, sewer construction, and other municipal services. A municipal council has no decision-making powers, and municipal officials are subject to numerous legal, financial, and political limitations imposed by national officials. The members of the council vary in number from five to 17, according to the population of the local entity.

Electoral System: Venezuela has universal suffrage at 18 years of age. The president is elected by popular vote for a six-year term. The last presidential elections were held on July 30, 2000. Of 11,681,645 registered voters, 6,600,196 votes were cast, or 56.5 percent of registered voters. Hugo Chávez Frías won with 3,757,773 votes, or 56.9 percent of votes cast; Lieutenant Colonel Francisco Arias Cárdenas placed second with 2,359,459 votes, or 35.7 percent of the votes cast. A special presidential recall vote on August 15, 2004, resulted in a victory for Chávez, who won 58 percent of the vote in favor of his fulfilling the remaining two years of his term; 42 percent voted in favor of terminating his presidency immediately. Presidential elections are next scheduled for mid-2006. Legislative elections were last held on July 30, 2000. The next legislative elections are due in 2005. The next municipal elections are slated for 2009.

Politics and Political Parties: In early 2005, President Chávez's Fifth Republic Movement (Movimiento Venezolano Quinta República—MVR) remained the dominant party within the National Assembly, with 68 of 165 seats, as a result of the July 2000 elections. The once-dominant Venezuelan party, Democratic Action (Acción Democrática—AD), remained in second place, with 24 seats. Parties holding 11 seats or fewer include the Movement Toward Socialism (Movimiento al Socialismo—MAS), Project Venezuela (Proyecto Venezuela—PV), Justice First (Primero Justicia—PJ), AD-Social Christian Party (Comité de Organización Política Electoral Independiente—COPEI) Alliance (Alianza AD-COPEI), Radical Cause (Casua Radical—CR), National Indian Council of Venezuela (Consejo Nacional Indio de Venezuela—Conive), and New Party (Partido Nuevo—PN). The center-right PJ has both kept its distance from the discredited traditional parties and engaged in strong opposition to the government.

Chávez easily won the last presidential election and, despite crippling national strikes in 2002–3, scored a major victory in the special presidential recall vote of August 2004. International electoral observers ratified the referendum results, but opponents charged that the use of untested electronic voting machines allowed fraud to take place. Chávez's victory validated the legitimacy of his rule until January 2007, but he could continue in power until 2012 because he is eligible to run as a candidate in the presidential election scheduled for 2006. Since President Chávez's impressive victory in the referendum, tensions in the country have abated, but the political environment remains highly polarized. Three other factors in particular also weigh in his favor: pro-Chávez candidates won in 20 of the country's 22 states in the regional elections for state governors and mayors on October 31, 2004; the pro-Chávez faction within the National Assembly strengthened his control over the government in December 2004 by expanding the number of magistrates in the Supreme Tribunal of Justice (Tribuna Suprema de Justicia—TSJ) from 20 to 32, while appointing 17 new pro-Chávez judges and 32 potential substitutes to the TSJ; and the opposition remained in complete disarray in early 2005 and without any leader of comparable popular appeal.

Mass Media: The constitution provides for freedom of speech and of the press. According to the U.S. Department of State, the Chávez government had generally respected these rights in practice as of 2003. Nevertheless, press freedom reportedly deteriorated during 2003 with efforts by some individuals associated with the government to provoke, threaten, or physically harm or encourage others to attack private media owners, their installations, and journalists working for them. According to a 2000 telecommunications law, the government may order obligatory national broadcasts that pre-empt scheduled programming, a prerogative that the government has used excessively, according to domestic and international observers. In 2003 the government required all television and radio stations to air as many as 162 hours of speeches by President Chávez and government officials as well as other pro-government programming, compared with only 73 hours in 2002. In his annual message to the National Assembly in January 2003, President Chávez declared the "year of the war against the media."

Most radio and television stations and newspapers, both private and government-owned, reportedly have become heavily politicized since President Chávez came to power. Independent media observers have criticized the state media for partisan coverage of events, as well as for encouraging a climate of hostility toward the media that jeopardizes freedom of the press. State media employees have complained of purges of employees known to be anti-Chávez. The five main privately owned TV channels—CMT, Globovisión (a 24-hour news channel), Radio Caracas Televisión (RCTV), Televen, and Venevisión—and most of the 10 major national newspapers, including Caracas-based dailies *El Nacional* and *El Universal*, have directly supported the opposition campaigns against the Chávez government.

In December 2004, the government adopted a controversial media-content law that it said would improve broadcasting standards by prohibiting the inappropriate airing of scenes of sex and violence. However, critics of the bill, which also bans material deemed "contrary to national security," regard it as an attempt to silence media criticism. Two of the most prominent anti-Chávez journalists subsequently lost their jobs as television news anchors. Human Rights Watch, and the Inter American Press Association, Reporters Without Borders, and the U.S. government expressed concern about deteriorating press freedom in Venezuela in 2004 and early 2005. Under the new Penal Code signed by President Chávez on March 16, 2005, a person who "disrespects the president" could be punished with six to 30 months in prison (Article 147). Comments that "expose another person to contempt or public hatred" are punishable by one to three years of prison (Article 444). Someone who "causes public panic or anxiety" with inaccurate reports may be imprisoned for five years (Article 297a).

Foreign Relations: The ideological cornerstone of President Chávez's "Bolivarian" foreign policy is to build a "multipolar" world with regional alliances that would counterbalance U.S. domination of world affairs. As a founding member of the Organization of the Petroleum Exporting Countries (OPEC) and an especially active OPEC member under President Chávez, Venezuela has more extensive ties with the wider international community than most other countries in the region. In November 2001, Chávez traveled extensively throughout Europe and Africa in order to promote higher oil prices and his vision of a multipolar world. Although neighboring countries have responded coolly to Chávez's foreign policy and have shown little interest in his proposed South American military alliance, they greatly value economic relations with their wealthy OPEC neighbor.

Venezuela has long-standing territorial disputes with Guyana and Colombia, but it does not have a history of armed conflict with its neighbors. Relations with Colombia have been delicate since 1999, when President Chávez began criticizing Colombia's U.S.-funded antinarcotics strategy called Plan Colombia, which Chávez has opposed on the basis that it has resulted in incursions into Venezuela by displaced refugees and combatants. For its part, Colombia has been critical of the Chávez government for allowing Colombian guerrillas to use Venezuelan territory as a haven. Tensions between Colombia and Venezuela worsened in April 2003, when Colombia accused Venezuela of violating its airspace. Relations deteriorated again as a result of Venezuelan alarm over Colombia's projected purchase of tanks from Spain for deployment to the Guajira Peninsula bordering Venezuela. In July, after the new Spanish government suspended delivery of the tanks, a meeting held by the presidents of Colombia and Venezuela helped to repair bilateral relations, but only temporarily. Events surrounding the capture of

Rodrigo Granda, the foreign relations chief of the Revolutionary Armed Forces of Colombia in Caracas by agents of Colombia's government—allegedly with the paid cooperation of Venezuelan army personnel—in December 2004 reversed any warming in relations. Venezuela withdrew its ambassador from Bogotá on January 15, 2005, and relations between Venezuela and Colombia remained in the worst state of crisis in nearly two decades.

Trade dominates Venezuela's relations with Brazil. In February 2005, the two countries signed energy and mining accords that permit the Brazilian Petroleum Corporation to develop offshore natural gas projects and oil fields in eastern Venezuela's Orinoco Heavy Oil Belt. Venezuela's apparent inability or unwillingness to clamp down on cross-border drug trafficking or to improve security along its remote Amazonian border has been of concern to the Brazilians.

Cuba is the Chávez government's closest ally, and both governments benefit greatly from this relationship. Venezuela is an important source of oil for Cuba. Chávez visited Cuba three times in 2004. As of February 2005, Cuba reportedly had 20,000 doctors, dentists, teachers, and sports trainers in Venezuela, mainly working in poor pro-Chávez neighborhoods of Caracas. Fidel Castro pledged in early 2005 that the number of Cubans would increase to 30,000 by the end of the year. In 2004 President Chávez reportedly posted dozens of Cuban "advisers" to the internal security and immigration agencies of the Ministry of Interior and Justice, other key ministries, and the Central Bank.

U.S.-Venezuelan relations have been strained since Chávez came to power in early 1999. President Chávez's criticism of the U.S. bombing campaign in Afghanistan in November 2001 as "terrorism" especially irked the White House. The Chávez government's relations with the United States, Colombia, and Spain have been particularly tense since the abortive coup attempt in April 2002, which these countries appeared to welcome. Chávez also accused the United States of being behind the coup attempt. Relations with the United States have been further strained over Chávez's denunciation of the planned Free Trade Area of the Americas (FTAA), his strident opposition to the U.S. conduct of the global "war on terrorism," and his close trading ties and relations with Cuba and Iran. Chávez viewed U.S. sympathy for the opposition in the August 2004 referendum as another example of U.S. meddling in Venezuela's internal affairs. Despite this troubled relationship, pragmatic economic considerations take precedence in U.S.-Venezuelan relations because of the significance of oil.

Membership in International Organizations: Venezuela has membership or observer status in the Agency for the Prohibition of Nuclear Weapons in Latin America and the Caribbean, Andean Pact, Andean Community of Nations, Caribbean Community and Common Market (observer), Caribbean Development Bank, Food and Agriculture Organization, Group of 3, Group of 15, Group of 24, Group of 77, Inter-American Development Bank, International Atomic Energy Agency, International Bank for Reconstruction and Development (World Bank), International Chamber of Commerce, International Civil Aviation Organization, International Confederation of Free Trade Unions, International Criminal Court, International Criminal Police Organization, International Federation of Red Cross and Red Crescent Societies, International Finance Corporation, International Fund for Agricultural Development, International Hydrographic Organization, International Labour Organisation, International Maritime Organization, International Monetary Fund, International Olympic Committee, International Organization for

Migration, International Organization for Standardization, International Red Cross and Red Crescent Movement, International Telecommunication Union, Latin American Economic System, Latin American Integration Association, Nonaligned Movement, Organisation for the Prohibition of Chemical Weapons, Organization of American States (OAS), Organization of the Petroleum Exporting Countries (OPEC), Permanent Court of Arbitration, Rio Group, Southern Cone Common Market (associate member), United Nations, UN Conference on Trade and Development, UN Educational, Scientific, and Cultural Organization, UN High Commissioner for Refugees, UN Industrial Development Organization, Universal Postal Union, World Confederation of Labor, World Customs Organization, World Federation of Trade Unions, World Health Organization, World Intellectual Property Organization, World Meteorological Organization, World Tourism Organization, and World Trade Organization.

Major International Treaties: Venezuela subscribes to various multilateral treaties and bilateral agreements that are designed to protect and promote international investment. It subscribes to 90 international environmental pacts, including the Antarctic Treaty and conventions on Biodiversity, Climate Change, Desertification, Endangered Species, Hazardous Wastes, Marine Life Conservation, Ozone Layer Protection, Ship Pollution, Tropical Timer 83, Tropical 94, and Wetlands. It has signed but not ratified the Kyoto Protocol. Venezuela also has signed and ratified a number of human rights treaties relating to racial discrimination and the rights and status of women and children. Venezuela has signed the Protocol to Prevent, Suppress, and Punish Trafficking in Persons and has signed (but not yet ratified) the Protocol against the Smuggling of Migrants. Treaties related to national security include the principal biological and chemical weapons treaties, the Nuclear Non-Proliferation Treaty, the Nuclear Test-Ban Treaty, and the Inter-American Treaty of Reciprocal Assistance of 1947 (Rio Treaty). In the area of terrorism and crime, Venezuela has ratified the Inter-American Convention Against Terrorism and the UN International Convention for the Suppression of the Financing of Terrorism. Venezuela is a party to numerous bilateral and multilateral narcotics-control agreements, including the 1988 UN Drug Convention. It honors its anti-drug money-laundering agreement with the United States, and the United States and Venezuela have an extradition treaty.

NATIONAL SECURITY

Armed Forces Overview: At the end of 2002, the government of President Hugo Chávez reorganized the armed forces into a unified force called the National Armed Force (Fuerza Armada Nacional—FAN). The president is commander in chief of the FAN. The president's authority is exercised through the minister of national defense, who is normally a senior military officer, although the first civilian defense minister to hold the post in recent decades served from February 2001 to April 2002. The National Defense Council advises the president on national security matters, and the Higher Council of the Armed Forces, on defense matters.

Total armed forces strength in 2004 was 83,300. The 34,000-member "Forger of Freedoms" Venezuelan Army controls the rest of the components of the FAN, including the 18,300-member Navy, the 7,000-member Venezuelan Air Force (Aviación Militar Venezolana—AMV), and 24,000-member National Guard of Venezuela (Guardia Nacional de Venezuela—GNV), whose formal name is the Armed Forces of Cooperation (Fuerzas Armadas de Cooperación—FAC).

Although an active branch of the military and subordinate to the minister of defense, the National Guard has arrest powers and is largely responsible for internal security, including maritime security, maintaining public order, guarding the exterior of key government installations and prisons, conducting counternarcotics operations, monitoring borders, and providing law enforcement in remote areas.

During 2003, the FAN reportedly became an increasingly politicized force under the new defense minister, a general, and has been restructured and purged of anyone suspected of political disloyalty to President Chávez. Those purged included senior National Guard officers who were at the forefront of the rebellion against President Chávez in April 2002. Although the previous constitution stated that the military was expected to be "apolitical, obedient, and non-deliberating," the 1999 constitution states only that the military should be "without militancy." The new constitution also gives the president the authority to make military promotions without legislative approval and allows the military the right to vote. Moreover, the military presence within the Chávez government is extensive. Numerous active-duty and retired officers have been appointed to replace civilians in high-ranking positions in central and regional government institutions and state-owned companies. In 2003 five of the 14 presidential cabinet members had previously served in the military, and in January 2005 two ministers, including the minister of defense, were active-duty generals.

Foreign Military Relations: As the Chávez government has increased its security ties with Cuba, it has reduced Venezuela's traditionally close military and security ties with the United States. For example, in March 2004 Venezuela withdrew its military contingent from the U.S. Army's Western Hemisphere Institute for Security Cooperation (the former School of the Americas), in Fort Benning, Georgia. In the interest of diversification, the Chávez government has sought to develop military relations with China, Cuba, Russia, and Ukraine. China's defense minister visited Venezuela for the first time in September 2001. Venezuela signed a military cooperation agreement with Russia in 2001. The arrangement facilitates the acquisition by Venezuela of Russian military aircraft or helicopters and other weapons. Some Cuban advisers reportedly have been posted in the Ministry of Defense's General Directorate for Military Intelligence (Dirección de Inteligencia Militar—DIM), and some Cuban military advisers reportedly are engaged in training the military. In early 2005, Venezuela's National Assembly ratified a 1999 security agreement with Cuba that is intended to facilitate cooperation between security personnel in Venezuela and Cuba.

External Threat: The greatest external security threat to Venezuela is the spillover of the conflict in Colombia. The Colombian insurgency and counterinsurgency fighting have caused refugee flows and the spread of violence by left-wing insurgent and paramilitary right-wing groups operating in border areas, as well as the spread of organized drug trafficking and extortion. Although Venezuela is a signatory to the Rio Treaty, the Chávez government views it as anachronistic and has proposed replacing it with a regional solution in the form of a South American military alliance.

The Chávez government apparently now sees the United States as its principal adversary. Now closely allied with Fidel Castro Ruz of Cuba, President Chávez reportedly has ordered Venezuela's armed forces to implement a new Cuban-style strategy in which the top priority is preparing to fight a war of resistance against an invasion by the United States. In addition, Chávez has ordered a doubling of the army's reserve, to more than 100,000 troops under his personal command. "Popular defense units" of 50 to 500 civilians are to be established in workplaces and on farms.

Defense Budget: In 2003 military expenditures were slightly more than US$1.1 billion, or 1.3 percent of gross domestic product (GDP), as compared with US$1.2 billion in 2002, a figure that amounted to US$50 per capita, 1.8 percent of GDP, and US$15,227 per member of the armed forces.

Major Military Units: The army is organized into five infantry divisions, one corps of engineers, and one reserve corps. The infantry divisions include 15 brigades (armored, 1; cavalry, 1; light armored, 1; infantry, 7; airborne, 1; Ranger, 2; mobile, 1; counterguerrilla, 1; and military police, 1); and 3 regiments (aviation, 1; and engineering, 2). The navy is organized into western and eastern naval zones and four commands: naval aviation, coast guard, fleet, and riverine. In addition, the 5,000-member Venezuelan Marine Corps (Infantería de Marina Venezolana—IMV), which engages in riverine operations against drug traffickers, is subordinate to the navy. The air force is organized into four operational commands: air, air defense, logistics, and personnel.

Major Military Equipment: The armed forces are well equipped by regional standards. Their inventory includes 601 armored vehicles, 74 combat aircraft, and 8 naval vessels. The army has 81 AMX-30 tanks, 191 light tanks (75 M-18, 35 AMX-13, and 80 Scorpion 90s), 30 M-8 reconnaissance vehicles, 255 armored personnel carriers (APCs), 92 towed artillery pieces, 10 self-propelled artillery pieces, 20 multiple rocket launchers, 225 mortars, 24 antitank guided weapons, 175 recoilless launchers, 192 aircraft, and 26 helicopters (7 attack, 13 transport, and 6 support). The navy has six frigates, six frigates with area surface-to-air missiles, two submarines, six support and miscellaneous craft, six patrol and coastal combatants, three missile craft, three offshore patrol craft, four amphibious craft, three combat aircraft, and nine armed helicopters. The Marine Corps has 11 landing craft, 25 APCs, 18 towed artillery pieces, and six air defense guns. The coast guard has 2 offshore patrol craft and 16 inshore patrol craft. The air force has 125 combat aircraft and 31 armed helicopters, as well as 15 reconnaissance aircraft, 3 electronic countermeasures aircraft, 23 liaison aircraft, and 57 training aircraft. The National Guard has 20 armored infantry fighting vehicles, 24 APCs, 150 mortars, 14 small aircraft, 26 helicopters, and 52 inshore patrol craft.

Venezuela traditionally purchased much of its military equipment from the United States. U.S. foreign military sales to Venezuela in 2002 totaled US$20 million. However, Venezuela increasingly is turning to other countries for military equipment. In April 2004, Venezuela's Ministry of Defense embarked on a US$2-billion arms-acquisition program and subsequently signed an agreement, which was expanded later in the year, with Russia for various armaments for the army. In February 2005, Venezuela also was evaluating Russian MiG-29 fighters as replacements for its U.S.-made F-16s and seeking to purchase 24 Super Tucano multipurpose fighter aircraft from Brazil. In January 2005, Spain agreed to sell Venezuela up to four offshore patrol boats or light corvettes and a number of Casa military transport aircraft. In September 2004, Ukraine began providing light to medium military equipment to Venezuela, and negotiations were underway for Ukraine to supply more sensitive and strategically important military equipment.

Military Service: Military service of 24 to 30 months is in theory compulsory for all male citizens from the age of 18, but in practice the draft system is selective. Only about 20,000 conscripts are serving at any given time, out of an estimated pool of 250,730 males who reach military age annually, and an estimated total pool of 4,953,803 males who are between the ages of 15 and 49 and deemed fit for military service. On completion of their term of military training, many conscripts choose to enlist in the National Guard, which is a voluntary force.

Military Forces Abroad: Participation in international peacekeeping missions is part of the Venezuelan Army's mission statement. In 2002 Venezuela contributed slightly less than US$1 million to United Nations peacekeeping operations, as compared with Argentina and Brazil, which each contributed about US$10 million. Venezuela is a member of the UN Military Observer Force in Pakistan and India and the UN Iraq-Kuwait Observer Mission and has contributed to the UN Peacekeeping Force in Haiti.

Security Forces: Police forces are organized at the national, state, and municipal levels. At the national level, the two main investigative forces are the Directorate of Intelligence and Prevention Services (Dirección de los Servicios de Inteligencia y Prevención—Disip), an internal security force under the Ministry of Interior and Justice that is responsible for dealing with crimes against the state, such as subversion, arms smuggling, narcotics trafficking, and kidnapping; and the Judicial Technical Police (Cuerpo Técnico de Policía Judicial—PTJ), which also is under the Ministry of Interior and Justice and is responsible for investigating federal crimes not already covered by the Disip. Another agency that is responsible for collecting intelligence related to national security is the General Directorate for Military Intelligence (Dirección de Inteligencia Militar—DIM), which is controlled by the Ministry of Defense. The National Guard also serves as a federal police force. It has arrest powers and is largely responsible for maintaining public order. The internal security role of the armed forces was strengthened in September 2002 when President Chávez decreed 107 security zones in the national territory, including eight in Caracas. Until then, the armed forces traditionally had security zones only in the border areas. National Guard or police members man the countrywide police checkpoints, which are common on the roads outside cities.

State- and municipal-level police forces include the following: Metropolitan Police; Municipal Police; Transport Police, under the Ministry of Interior and Justice; and Traffic Police, under the Transportation Ministry. Each state has a uniformed police force, which is partly regulated by the local Police Code. However, there are proposals to merge these state forces into a single national force. Municipal mayors and state governors are responsible for local and state police forces, which maintain independence from the central government. Urban police entities are under the command of National Guard officers. The Caracas Metropolitan Police is the main civilian police force in the five municipalities or departments that form the capital district and is headed by a career police officer, rather than a military officer. Civilian authorities generally maintain control over security forces, but individual members of the security forces reportedly have committed numerous and serious human rights abuses. Vigilante groups formed by police officers have been linked to an average 10 killings a month since 2001.

The number of police in 2004 totaled 26,000 (state, municipal, and metropolitan police forces: 18,000; Disip: 3,000; PTJ: 3,000; and Traffic Police: 2,000). Venezuela has 505 police officers per 100,000 inhabitants. Although this ratio compares favorably with other countries, public confidence in the police is low, and the density of police officers varies widely. For example, the wealthy Caracas municipality of Chacao has 1,228 policemen per 100,000, whereas the city's poor municipality of Libertador has only 63 per 100,000.

In addition to the official security forces, Chávez has distributed weapons to the estimated 10,000 members of the Bolivarian Circles, independently organized groups of Chávez supporters at the grassroots level of Venezuelan society. These groups are modeled on Cuba's Committees for the Defense of the Revolution and operate in groups of between seven and 11 people.

Internal Threat: In contrast to neighboring Colombia, Venezuela does not have any insurgent or terrorist groups seeking to overthrow the government. Venezuela does, however, suffer spillover violence from Colombia. Since 2001, the number of incidents of extortion and kidnapping perpetrated by Colombian armed groups against ranchers in the border states of Venezuela has been increasing, and Colombian right-wing paramilitary forces also have been using the Venezuelan border areas for logistical support since early 2003. Venezuelan security forces have clashed repeatedly with the various armed Colombian groups operating in the border region, but the security situation has continued to deteriorate. The ranchers, who are generally strong opponents of Chávez, have complained about having to supply National Guard troops with food and fuel in order to receive protection.

Crime levels in Venezuela are more comparable to those in Colombia, with the main exception of kidnappings, which are not nearly as common in Venezuela as in Colombia. Violent crime is a major problem in the largest cities, in particular Caracas, which has one of the highest crime rates in South America. Venezuela's homicide rate has increased sharply since the early 1990. More than 11,000 murders were reported in 2003, as compared with only 2,000 in 1991. In a terrorist-like incident unusual for Venezuela, the controversial public prosecutor, Danilo Anderson, who answered directly to President Chávez, was assassinated by a car bomb in Caracas in November 2004.

As of January 2005, two pro-Chávez leftist militant groups whose objective reportedly is to confront intervention by U.S. and other foreign forces were known to be operating in Venezuela. Chávez himself has acknowledged the existence of the 500-member Bolivarian Forces of Liberation (Fuerzas Bolivarianas de Liberación—FBL), which reportedly has been operating in the Venezuelan border area as a local kidnapping and extortion "franchise" of the Revolutionary Armed Forces of Colombia. The other pro-Chávez militant group is the Armed People's Army (Ejército del Pueblo en Armas—EPA), which emerged in January 2005.

Narcotics Production and Trafficking: Large quantities of cocaine, heroin, and marijuana transit the country from Colombia, bound for the United States and Europe. Increasing signs of drug-related activities by Colombian insurgents on the border and significant narcotics-related, money-laundering activity, especially along the border with Colombia and on Margarita Island, have been noted. Coca and opium poppy are cultivated along the Colombian border in small amounts, although Venezuela has an active eradication program, primarily targeting opium. In

2003 cocaine seizures increased dramatically, reaching 32 tons, nearly double previous year record seizures of 17.8 tons, according to figures provided by Venezuelan authorities. In 2003, for the fourth straight year, Venezuela led the continent in heroin seizures (about half a ton), ahead of Colombia. Venezuela received about US$4 million in U.S. international narcotics control and counterdrug funding in 2004 and about US$3.6 million in 2005.

Human Rights: Of the 350 articles in the 1999 constitution, 116 are dedicated to duties, human rights, and guarantees, including a chapter on the rights of the indigenous peoples. Nevertheless, according to the U.S. Department of State, the Chávez government's human rights record remains poor, having deteriorated further in 2004. This record is characterized by extrajudicial killings of criminal suspects committed by the police and military, alleged police links to vigilante death squads responsible for hundreds of killings in at least 11 states, and increasing numbers of arbitrary arrests and detentions. The harsh prison conditions are characterized by continuing torture and abuse of detainees and inhumane and degrading treatment resulting from violence and severe overcrowding. Meanwhile, impunity remains one of the country's most serious human rights problems; the government has failed to punish police and security officers guilty of abuses. Corruption, lengthy pretrial detention, and severe inefficiency in the judicial and law enforcement systems also are problems. Investigations into the forced disappearances by the security forces of criminal suspects are extremely slow. Crimes involving human rights abuses often do not proceed to trial as a result of judicial and administrative delays.

In the human rights report released on March 28, 2005, the U.S. Department of State reported that in 2004 the Chávez government increased its control over the judicial system and its interference in the administration of justice. The National Assembly passed a law in May that enabled it to pack the Supreme Tribunal of Justice with Chávez sympathizers and to exert greater control over the justices. Judicial harassment and baseless political prosecutions against opposition and nongovernmental organization leaders continued. Moreover, the new media law passed by the legislature in December erodes freedom of speech and promotes self-censorship by media owners. The Chávez government also has conducted illegal wiretapping of private citizens and intimidated political opponents.